BOOK 1

Musical IMPRESSIONS

11 Solos in a Variety of Styles for Early Elementary to Elementary Pianists

MARTHA MIER

Musical Impressions was written to provide pianists with the experience of playing in a variety of styles. Capturing the essence of different styles is an important aspect in the development of all pianists.

Jazz styles, romantic ballads, mysterious sounds, and more are found in this series. These pieces will appeal to pianists of any age who enjoy playing pieces with many different moods.

It is my wish that playing this music will aid in developing stylistic performances in all students, leaving them with lasting *Musical Impressions*!

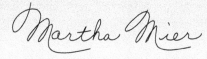

Contents

Alfred Music
P.O. Box 10003
Van Nuys, CA 91410-0003
alfred.com

ISBN-10: 1-4706-3328-0
ISBN-13: 978-1-4706-3328-8

Cover Photo:
AutumnMusicBackground © istockphoto / Rkaulitzki

Chocolate Smoothie

Martha Mier

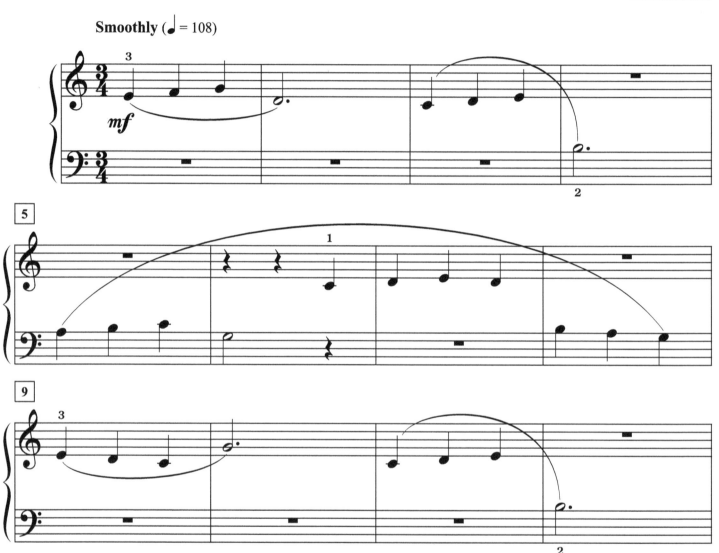

Optional Duet Accompaniment (Student plays one octave higher.)

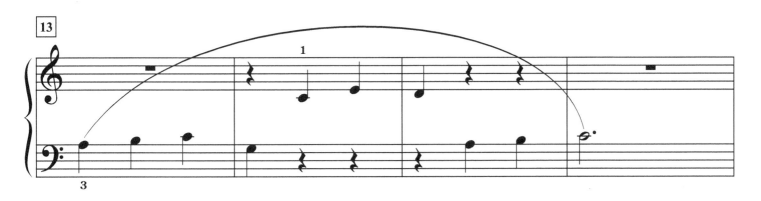

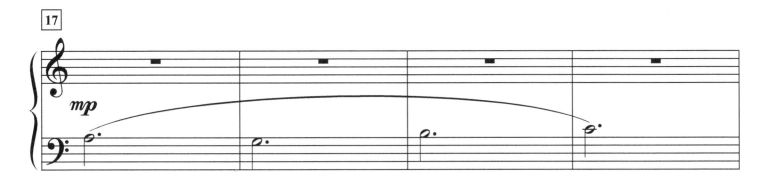

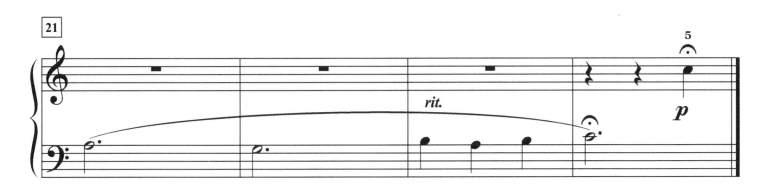

Castle by the Sea

Martha Mier

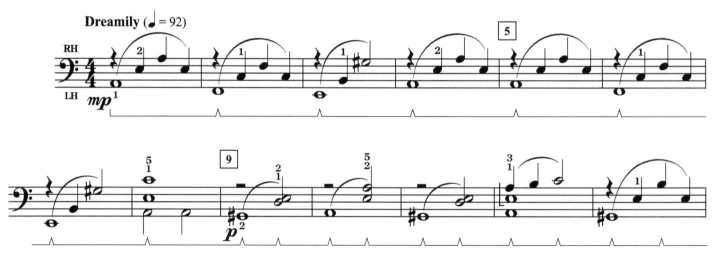

Optional Duet Accompaniment (Student plays one octave higher.)

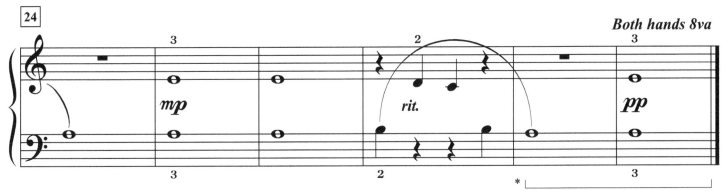

* When played as a duet, the student does not pedal.

Armadillo Rag

Martha Mier

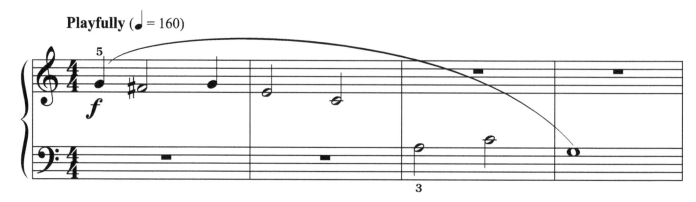

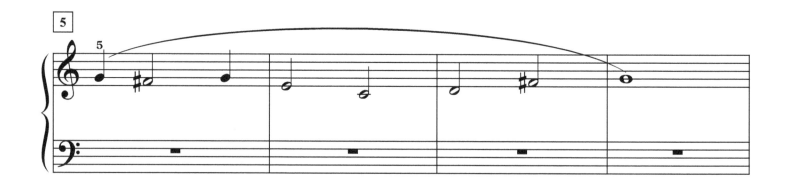

Optional Duet Accompaniment (Student plays one octave higher.)

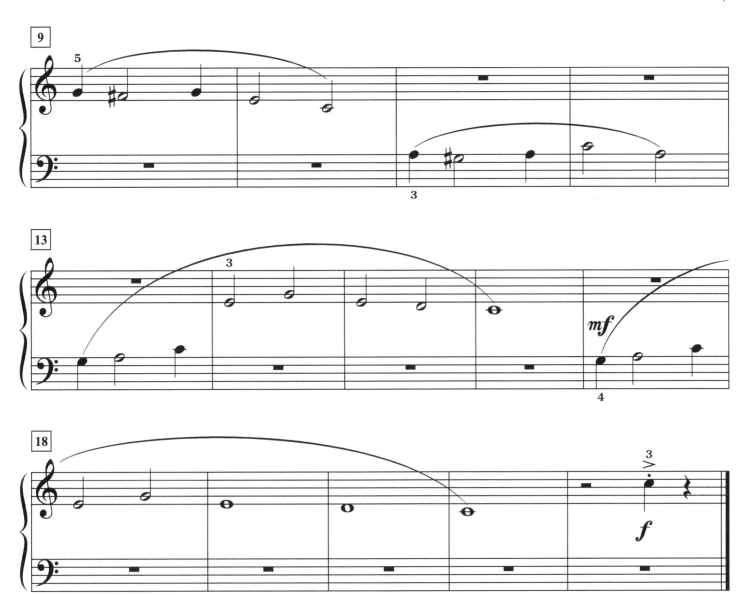

Drum Beats

Martha Mier

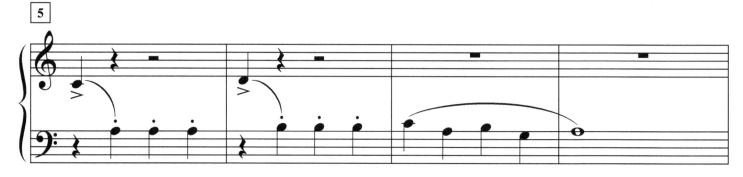

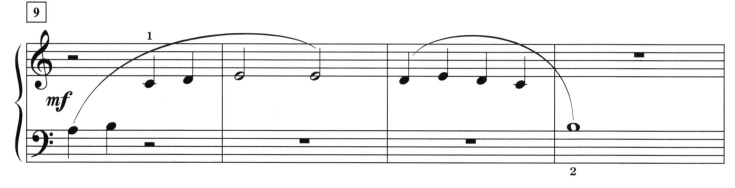

Optional Duet Accompaniment (Student plays one octave higher.)

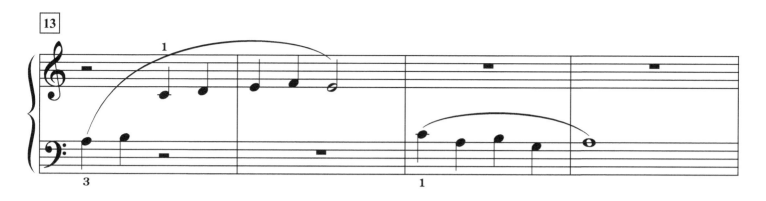

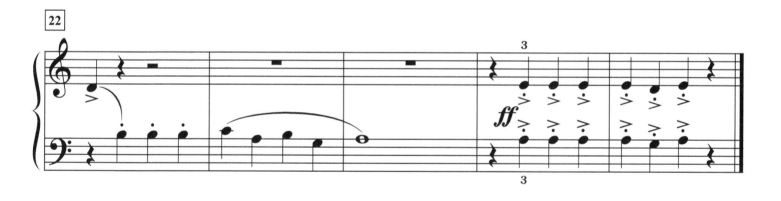

Hot Air Balloon Ride

Martha Mier

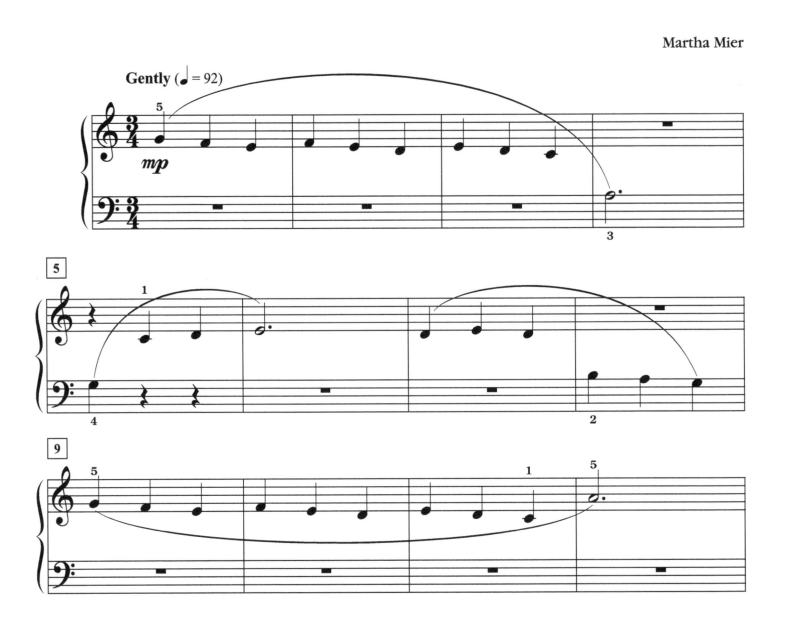

Optional Duet Accompaniment (Student plays one octave higher.)

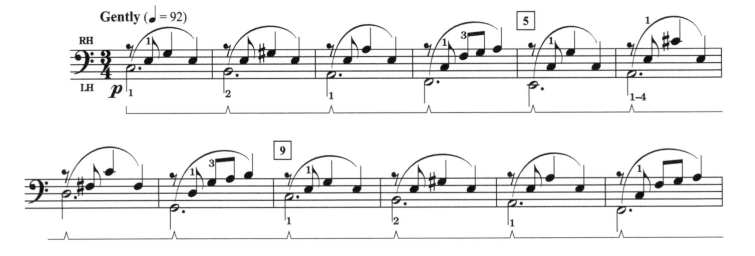

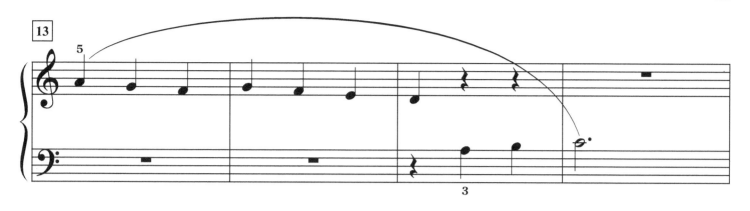

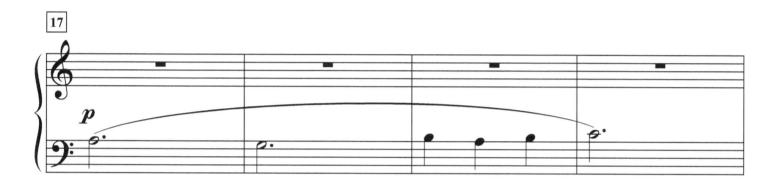

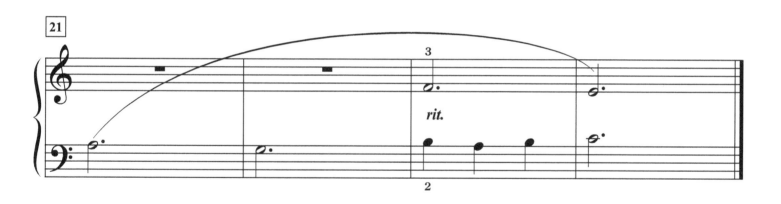

Butterflies and Rainbows

Martha Mier

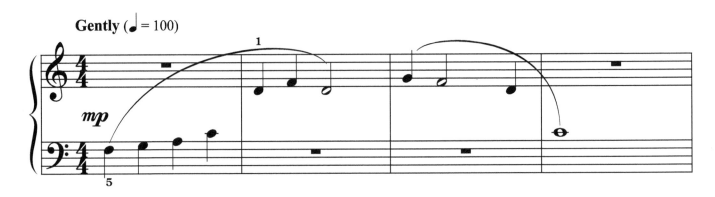

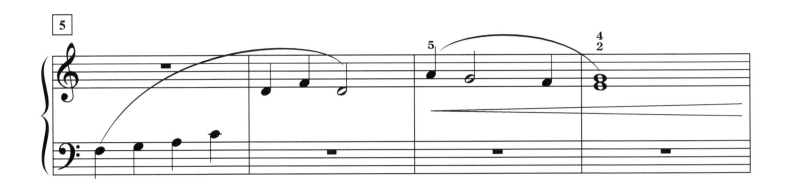

Optional Duet Accompaniment (Student plays one octave higher.)

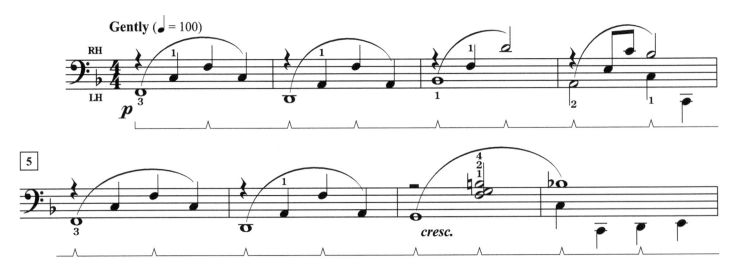

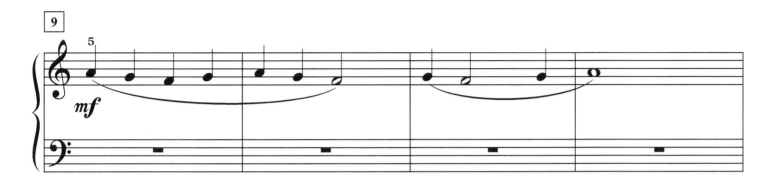

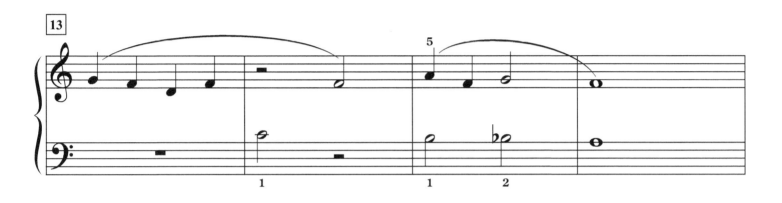

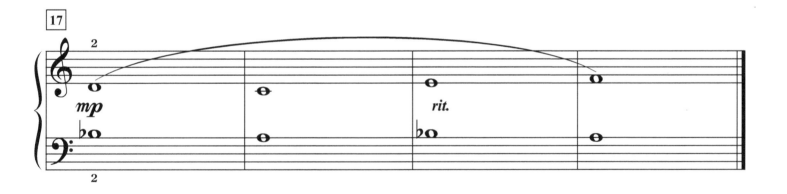

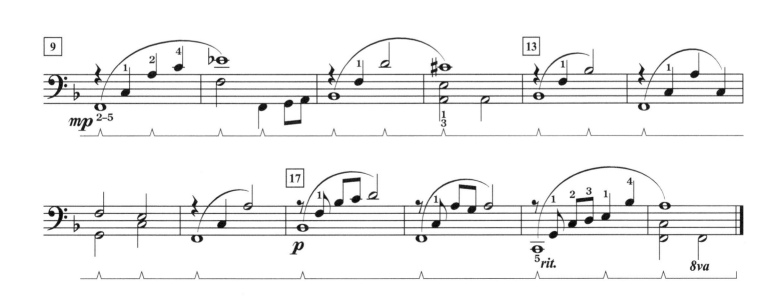

Hound Dog Blues

Martha Mier

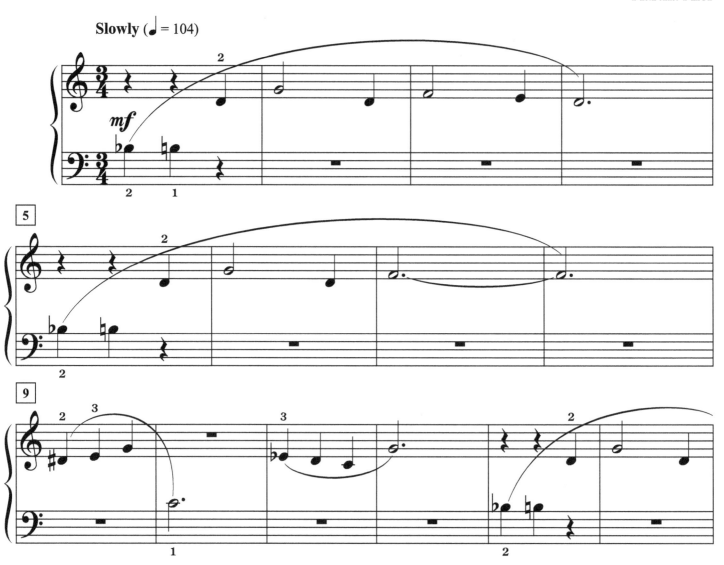

Optional Duet Accompaniment (Student plays one octave higher.)

* When played as a duet, the student does not pedal.

Whistle-Stop Boogie

Martha Mier

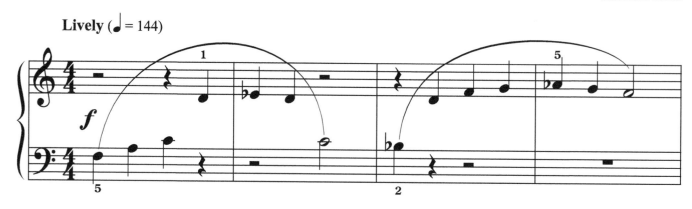

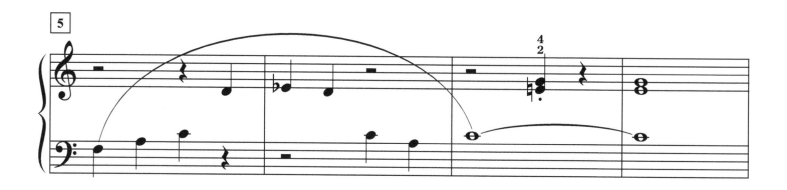

Optional Duet Accompaniment (Student plays one octave higher.)

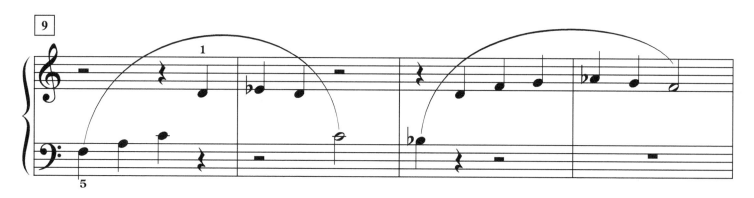

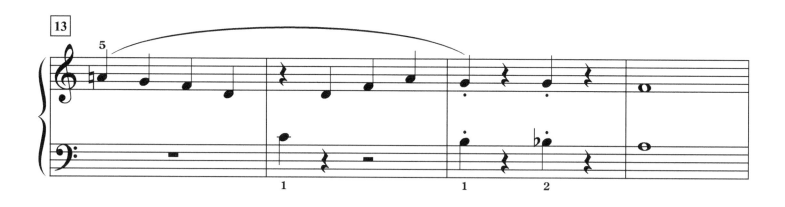

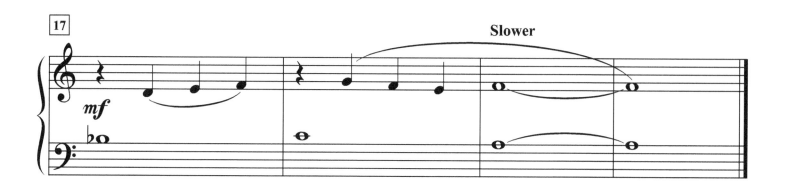

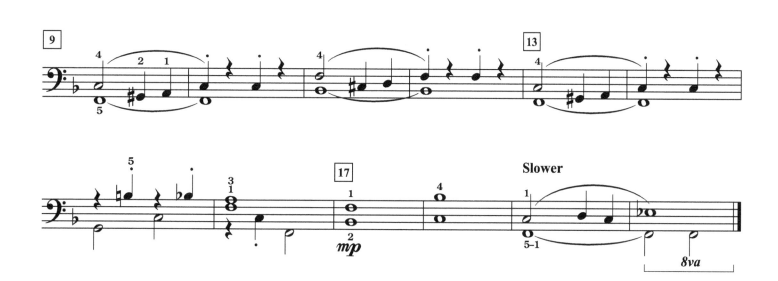

What's That Noise?

Martha Mier

Optional Duet Accompaniment (Student plays as written.)

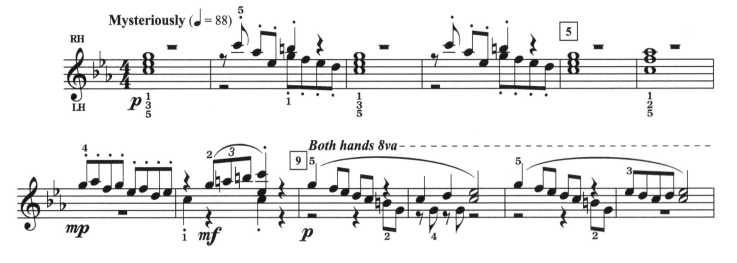

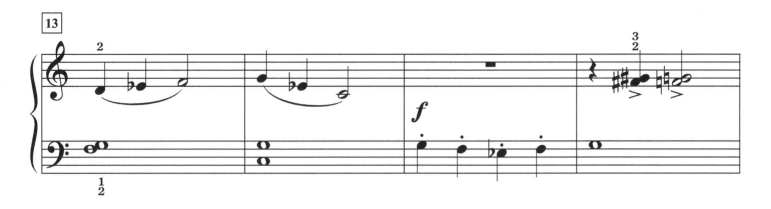

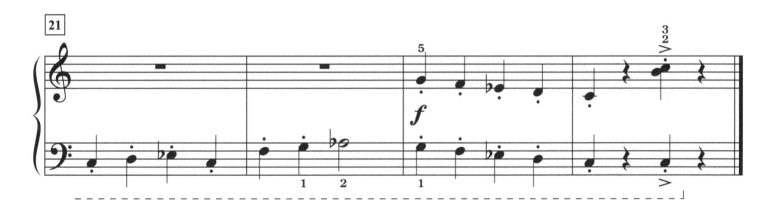

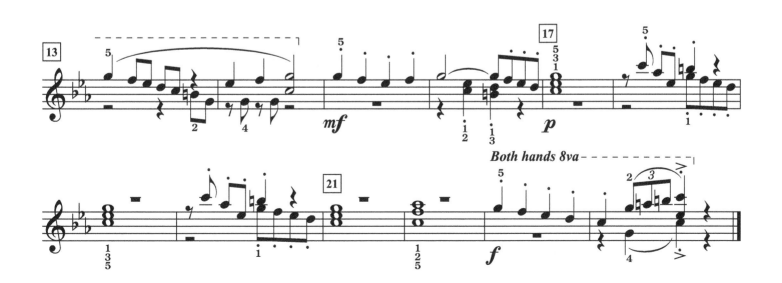

Mariachi Band

Martha Mier

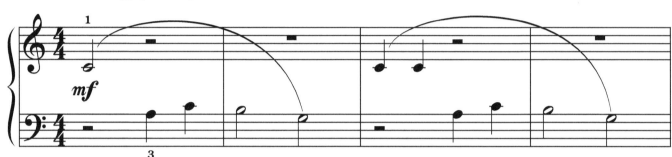

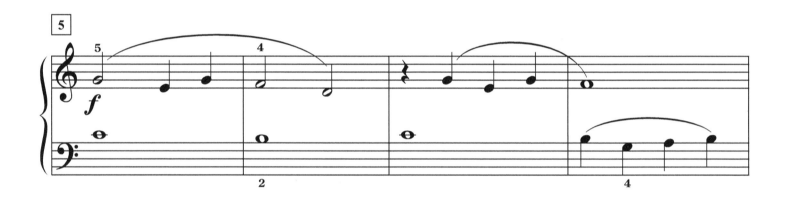

Optional Duet Accompaniment (Student plays one octave higher.)

Brazilian Maracas

Martha Mier

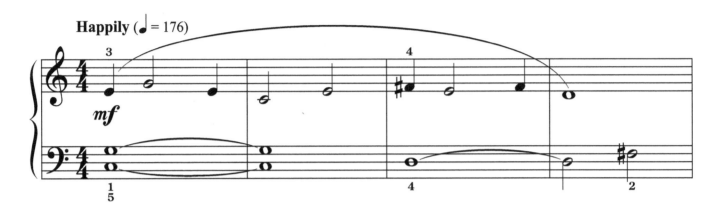

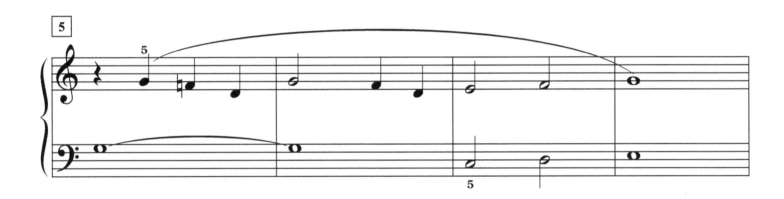

Optional Duet Accompaniment (Student plays one octave higher.)

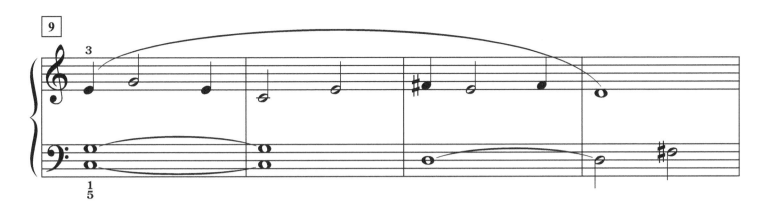

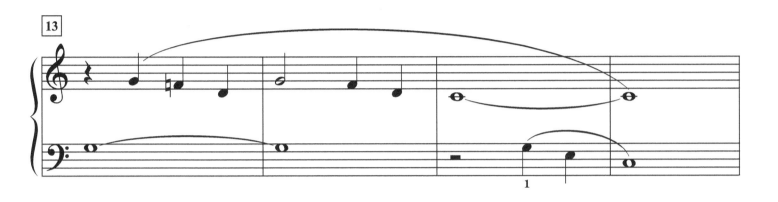

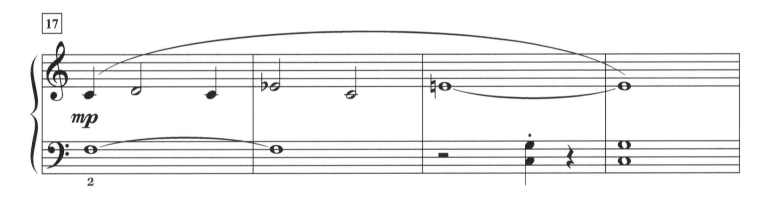

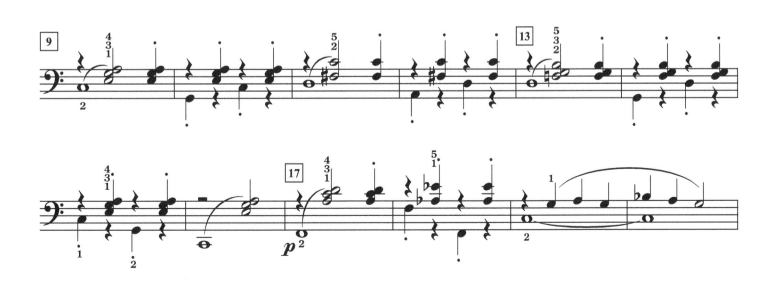

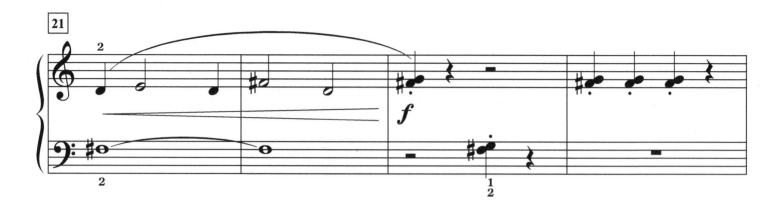

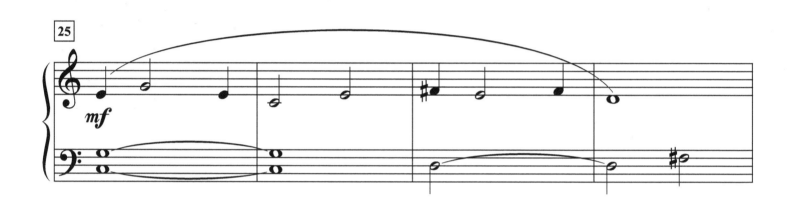

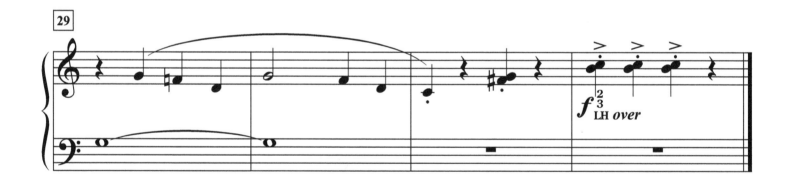

Optional Duet Accompaniment (continued)